Emotional Intelligence

How They Determine Our Success
Increase Your EQ by Mastering Your Emotions

Dan Miller

Legal Disclaimer

Table of Contents

Important Insight

Everyone is confronted by our own emotions in addition to those of other people. The manner in which we manage these emotions will determine how other people perceive us and our effectiveness in getting things done. By increasing our emotional intelligence, we will be better equipped to respond to situations around us with a high degree of maturity.

Studies by renowned researchers such as John Mayer, Peter Salovey and Konstantin Vasily Petrides have shown that people who have a high emotional intelligence become better leaders and are exemplary in whatever they do.

In his doctoral thesis entitled - *A study of Emotion: Developing Emotional Intelligence*, Wayne Payne became the first person to use the term emotional intelligence. Compared to intelligence quotient (IQ), emotional intelligence appears to be superior because it covers a wide range of faculties and aspects of people's behavior.

Studying emotional intelligence will help you understand the source and impact of your emotions. This is important because it enhances self awareness. You will also have an opportunity to understand the behavior of other people and the underlying reasons why they act the way they do.

Conflict management borrows heavily from emotional intelligence. By understanding the emotional needs of other people, you will be better placed to handle conflicts and resolve them in a manner that benefits every party. When conflicts are resolved amicably, they give you an opportunity to establish even stronger relationships and social bonds. A mastery of interpersonal skills such as listening, verbal communication, non-verbal communication, self management and assertiveness will make you gain trust and respect from others thereby becoming an influential person in social circles.

1: What Is Emotional Intelligence?

Emotional intelligence refers to the ability to identify, understand, use and manage emotions in a positive manner so as to enhance communication, relieve stress, overcome challenges, empathize with others and defuse conflict. The scope of emotional intelligence is wide and covers many different aspects of our daily lives such as the way in which we behave and interact with others.

An emotional intelligent person is able to recognize his own emotional state as well as the emotional states of other people. This makes him attractive and draws other people towards him. Having a clear understanding of the emotional states of the people you interact with will help you to relate well with them, achieve greater success at the workplace, form healthier relationships and lead a more satisfying life.

Compared to intelligence quotient (IQ), emotional intelligence is considered more important in attaining happiness and success in life and career. Our ability to read and interpret other people's signals and respond appropriately to them determines how far we can go in our individual and professional pursuit of success.

It is therefore important that every one of us develop a mature emotional intelligence framework that will help us to understand, negotiate and empathize with others. This is particularly important because the world is becoming increasingly interconnected and as such we are constantly exposed to cultural shocks from different parts of the globe.

Categories of Emotional Intelligence

Researchers in the area of emotional intelligence recognize the existence of five major classes of emotional intelligence skills.

Self-Awareness

Self-awareness is the ability to recognize your emotions and the impact they have on your thoughts and behavior. Through self-awareness, you will be able to understand your strengths and weaknesses. This is a critical component of your emotional intelligence complex and it helps you in building self-confidence.

Self-Regulation

The ability to put impulsive behaviors and feelings under control is another crucial part of emotional intelligence. While self-management does not necessarily prevent the occurrence of an emotion, it enables us to have a say in how long an emotion lasts. Learning how to manage emotions in a healthy way, adapting to changing circumstances and following through on commitments are some of the key aspects of self-regulation.

There are a number of techniques that you can use to ward off negative emotions such as anxiety, anger or depression. Some of these techniques include meditation and recasting situations in a positive light. Self-regulation involves the following attributes:

Self-control

This trains you on how to manage disruptive impulses.

Trustworthiness

This attribute of self-regulation enables you to maintain standards of integrity and honesty.

Conscientiousness

This refers to your ability to take responsibility for your own actions.

Adaptability

This component gives you flexibility in the face of changing circumstances.

Innovation

This a progressive attribute of self-regulation that opens you up to new ideas.

Motivation

Motivation refers to an internal process that propels you toward a goal. This category of emotional intelligence requires that you set clear goals, have a definite pathway and a positive attitude. Every one of us has a predisposition towards a negative or positive attitude but with motivation, we can shift how we think to a more positive orientation.

Every negative thought that may cross your mind at one point or another can be reframed in positive terms in order to help you achieve your goals. Motivation consists of:

Achievement Drive

This refers to a constant strive aimed at meeting a standard of excellence.

Commitment

This element of motivation aligns you with your personal or organizational goals.

Initiative

This describes your readiness to take advantage of opportunities that you come across.

Optimism

This refers to an incessant pursuit of goals despite setbacks and obstacles.

Empathy

Your ability to understand the needs, concerns and emotions of other people is an important element of emotional intelligence. Empathy enables you to recognize emotional cues and group power dynamics which in turn help you to respond appropriately to the reactions of other people. Empathetic people excel at:

Service Orientation

They are able to anticipate, recognize and meet the needs of others.

Developing Others

They can proactively sense deficiencies in other people and plug in so as to bolster their abilities.

Leveraging Diversity

Empathy leverages on the diversities expressed by others and create opportunities out of them.

Political Awareness

Empathy gives you the ability to read the emotional currents of a group and the powerful relationships that exists.

Social Skills

This is the last category of emotional intelligence but it is by no means the least. Social skills, also referred to as relationship management is the development of interpersonal skills that boost chances of success in life and career. Being a global economy with ease of access to information and technical knowledge, having people skills is important if we are to understand, empathize, inspire and work well in team settings.

In addition to conflict management, social skills enable you to:

Influence Others

Relationship management can make you persuasive enough to affect the behavior of other people.

Communicate

Social skills make it easier to pass messages across to people in a clear and concise manner.

Lead Others

By inspiring and guiding others, you can lead them in whichever direction you choose to.

Build Bonds

Through relationship management, you can create and nurture relationships that are beneficial to your personal and corporate development.

Collaborate and Cooperate – In order to succeed, you should work with others. This aspect of social skills enables you to harmoniously join forces with others towards a defined goal.

Psychologists agree that IQ alone is not sufficient in achieving happiness and success in life. According to their findings, IQ accounts for approximately 10 to 25 percent while emotional intelligence (EQ) accounts for 75 percent and above.

Other studies have also revealed that people with high EQ scores perform better at the work setting, are more self-confident and make better leaders. All these factors lead us to the conclusion that EQ is important and can enhance productivity and personal development.

2: Benefits of Emotional Intelligence

In today's competitive environment, having a high level of emotional intelligence can set you apart and create real opportunities for you. There are many benefits that can accrue as a result of having a high emotional intelligence (EQ). The good news is that every person who is ready and willing to increase their EQ levels can do so with good training.

It is in the public domain that people who are smart are not necessarily successful and fulfilled in life. For instance, there are people who are brilliant in academics but when it comes to personal relationships, they are inept. This is because such people have a high intelligence quotient but low levels of emotional intelligence.

There are many things that emotional intelligence can help you to attain and some of them include:

Personal Effectiveness

Emotional intelligence is regarded as a key ingredient in personal success. It gives you the ability to manage your affairs and those of others successfully. Emotional intelligence equips you with tools and strategies that make you more aware of yourself and teach you how to manage your emotions, both the positive and the negative. This increases your personal effectiveness.

Thinking Skills

What makes a problem difficult to solve may not be necessarily its complexity but rather the perspective that you have. Old difficulties can be solved by replacing old perspectives with new perspectives. Emotional intelligence also helps in developing your strategic thinking capacity and your ability to inspire and motivate your team.

Professional Relationships

Through emotional intelligence, you will understand what makes people tick. This is crucial in developing a harmonious and positive working environment and relationships. By boosting your emotional intelligence, your ability to interact and communicate more effectively with others will also go up. This in turn will enhance your professional relationships.

Leadership Capability

Effective leadership requires that you understand and empathize with the people that you lead.

Emotional intelligence equips you with strategies that are crucial in influencing, persuading, motivating and inspiring your subjects. The greatest determinant of success in any leadership and management style is the extent to which you understand the emotions of other people and how well you respond to them. This can enhance satisfaction and create a conductive environment for stronger workplace relationships.

If your response as a leader matches the expectations of the people you lead, then everyone will feel accommodated. You are likely to experience little if any resistance.

Physical Well-Being

As human beings, our emotional intelligence has a significant impact on our overall well-being. Stress management, which is closely tied to our emotional state, gives us the unique ability to react in a positive way even as we pass through storms of life. This is important because stress can weaken our physical abilities, lower our immune system and ultimately decrease the quality of life.

Mental Well-Being

Our attitude and outlook on life is shaped by emotional intelligence. If your EQ levels are low, you are likely to experience anxiety, depression and mood swings. This will in turn erode your positivity and optimism making your life dull and unpleasant. Your mental stability is usually at its highest when all your faculties including your ability to understand and interpret your emotions are working right.

Conflict Management

Conflicts do occur at one point or another without a preamble. Your ability to resolve any conflict is dependent upon your level of understanding of the emotions of people involved. If you can successfully discern and empathize with the feelings and perspectives of the people in the conflict, it becomes easy to solve such situations or even prevent them from occurring. Emotional intelligence makes us better negotiators because it gives us insights into the desires and needs of the parties in contention. When you know the bone of contention, resolving a conflict becomes much easier.

Success

Our ability to focus on a goal is a sum total of our internal motivators and self confidence. Higher levels of emotional intelligence give us self discipline and keep us on course towards attaining our goal. In addition, EQ allows us to create better support networks, persevere with an incredible degree of resilience and overcome setbacks that stand between us and our success. An emotional intelligent person can delay instant gratification and focus on the long term benefits of a certain course of action which boosts his chances of success.

Even though the field of emotional intelligence is still attracting studies by different scholars, what is clear is that emotions play a significant role in enhancing the quality of our personal and professional lifestyles. The advancement in technology has helped us to master information but has not replaced our ability to learn and manage our emotions.

In light of the benefits discussed above, it is up to you as an individual to take the initiative and boost your emotional intelligence.

3: How to Identify and Deal with Emotional Triggers

Emotional triggers refer to feelings, thoughts and events that seem to evoke an automatic response from a person. The use of the word trigger is critical because the reaction occurs automatically without much self control. While it seems involuntary, the reality is that the reaction just like everything else we do is a matter of choice. In order to take control over how we respond to circumstances, we must learn how to identify our personal emotional triggers.

There are times when unexpected events happen that turn our world upside down on a day that would have otherwise been relatively uneventful. For instance, you could be driving while in a good mood only to hear a sentimental or sad song from your car radio that instantly changes your emotions. When such events happen, people react in different ways depending on their emotional triggers.

How to Identify Emotional Triggers

Unless we are able to correctly identify our triggers, they will consistently rule over our emotions as long as we live. Instead of letting minor inconveniences make you run for the hills, you need to take charge of your emotions by first conquering your personal stressors also called stress inducers.

Categories of Stressors

There are different groups of stressors and some of them are:

Emotional Stressors

These can also be considered as internal stressors. They include anxieties, fears as well as personality traits such as pessimism, suspiciousness and perfectionism. These stressors can distort your thinking or perception towards other people.

Family Stressors

This is a category of stressors that includes financial problems, relationship changes with your spouse, experiencing empty-nest syndrome and coping with unruly adolescents. These can trigger an emotional response.

Social Stressors

Social stressors come up as a result of our interaction with other members of the society. They include public speaking, parties and dating. Just like emotional stressors, social stressors are individualized.

Change Stressors

These are stressors that originate from important changes that happen in our lives. They include moving to a new location or job, getting married, adopting a child among many others.

Work Stressors

Work stressors have their origin in a workplace environment that is full of pressure. The stressors include unpredictable bosses, tight deadlines or endless tasks.

In addition to the above stressors, there are other categories of triggers such as decision, physical, disease, phobic, environmental and pain.

After going through the above stressors, you should then list down the main stressors that your life falls into. It is possible to find that some of your stressors fall into more than one category.

How to Deal with the Triggers

Once you have established the triggers and the categories, you need to devise a strategy on how to deal with them one at a time. Some of the common approaches in dealing with emotion triggers include:

Elimination

Some of the emotional triggers can be eliminated for good. For instance, if a certain residential community does not give you the peace of mind, you can decide to move to a new area and start a new life. This way, you will have completely eliminated the social stressors from your life. For the workplace, you can either ask for a transfer or look for another job. However, it must be pointed out that some of these stressors cannot be easily eliminated or their elimination can cause significant loss in your life. To deal with them, you have to resolve to other strategies.

Reducing the Strength of the Stressors

This is a good strategy because it enables you to co-exist with others and yet reduce the impact of the stressors. For instance, if loud music from the neighborhood is stopping you from concentrating on your tasks, you can consider investing in a pair of ear plugs. If you feel that your morning trip to work is stressing you because you have to drive for more than two hours in heavy traffic daily, you can consider other viable options such as mass traveling or even carpooling.

Coping

It is said that if you cannot beat them, join them. For a majority of the stressors, you may just have to live with them because eliminating them can be counter-productive. You need to come up with coping techniques that will enable you to be clearheaded and calm even under pressure. The sooner you master these techniques, the better you become and some of the stressors will no longer be threatening as they used to.

Talking to a Friend

If you have a trusted friend, one of the best ways to do is to approach them and communicate your feelings to them. This way, you can get encouragement, fresh ideas and the support you need to overcome the triggers. You should carefully consider the feedback that you receive from your support partner because it comes from an independent perspective. If you cannot find a person to open up to, you may consider joining a support network where people facing similar challenges meet and talk to one another. Such networks have life coaches who are experienced in dealing with issues around emotional upsets.

Staying Positive

Some of the emotional triggers have a severe impact on us because of our perspectives. If you are determined to stay positive, it is very unlikely that emotional triggers will take their toll on you. You may encounter situations that have a potential to trigger your emotions but because of your focus on positivity, such situations may not succeed in turning your world upside down.

As part of living a positive life, you should try as much as possible to fight off any tendencies of anxiety. Instead of focusing on the uncertainties of tomorrow or the troubles of yesterday, you can choose to stay in the present and make good of the opportunities available.

While each one of us is emotionally sensitive to a certain degree, learning how to manage those emotions and the triggers causing them is what makes us different.

4: Taking Responsibility and Setting Personal Boundaries

Whatever circumstances that happen to you, the bottom line is that you are ultimately responsible for your life. This is a principle that you must embrace if you are seeking happiness and success in your personal and professional life.

There is always a temptation to heap the blame for your misfortunes onto another person but that does not help you either, if anything it worsens the situation and sinks you deeper into irresponsibility. Taking responsibility for your actions, choices and direction in life is the most powerful and intelligent way of dealing with issues in life. The moment you stop taking responsibility, your perspective toward life will change and in most times you will see yourself as a failure because you have permitted the winds of blame and excuses to blow you hither and yon.

Individuals who take total responsibility for their lives, experience control and joy despite the circumstances around them. They are able to make sober decisions and choices because they fully understand that they will be accountable for the outcome of their choices. Even if events that are not within your control come your way, you have the power to determine how you will react to them. You can either make a disaster out of a situation or use it as a ladder to climb to a higher level.

How to Take Responsibility for Your Life

One of the critical components that you must accept in life is that you are in charge and no one will live your life for you. It does not matter how hard you try to convince people around you that the events happening in your life are not consequences of your actions, you will still have to go through them and face the consequences as they come. In order to remain in control and handle every situation that you come across with resolve and determination, you need to:

Avoid Placing Blames on Others

Whether you are alone or in a group with others, you need to listen to yourself as you speak. Try as much as you can to eliminate blame and excuses in your speech. The more you repeatedly play the blame track in your mind, the more you are shifting responsibilities that you should bear to others.

Take Feedback Seriously

At times, you may not be keen enough to hear your voice as you speak with other people. This is why accepting feedback from others is important. Some of the people you talk to may be observant and honest enough to tell you about your tendencies to shift blame. If you take such feedback seriously, it may constructively change you and your perception to life. It is almost natural for human beings to dissent to feedback that does not favor them. The more you reject other people's observations, the more you are likely to continue with your irresponsible tendencies to your own detriment.

Plan Your Life

Life is a sum total of all the decisions, plans and courses of action that we take on a day to day basis. By putting in place a plan on how you want your life to run, you can successfully take control of your future thereby eliminating the temptation of blaming others for things that you are responsible for. Your plan should be broken down into simple and achievable goals that you can measure your progress on.

Recognize Your Choices

In any given situation, you have the overall choice on how to respond. This is irrespective of the severity of the circumstances. It is possible to be locked away in an extraordinary prison but still maintain your mental sanity. You have the option to focus on something more positive than the situation you are currently in. This will help you to free your emotions and to a larger extent your entire being.

Do Not Rely On External Validation

Some individuals depend on the opinions of other people to determine whether they should feel happy or sad. This is rather unfortunate because there is always something negative that people will speak about you and if you are not careful, it can bring you down emotionally. Reliance on external validation makes you to surrender your personal responsibility for making yourself happy.

External validation is pleasant and everyone wants to be pampered by others but at the end of it all, you cannot be fully dependent on such validations for your happiness. Train yourself to follow your values and act according to them because this is the only way through which you can take control of your life and happiness.

Open Your Mind to New Ideas and Beliefs

It is commonly said that our minds are like parachutes; they work best when they are open. Your beliefs through which you perceive the world will determine whether you will take charge or invite others to control your life. At times, your failure to take responsibility lies in the limiting beliefs that you have as an individual. Unless you open up and consider new ideas and value systems, you may not change the way you reason and speak.

Learn to Forgive and Move On

One of the reasons we oftentimes give for our lack of success is the mistakes that others committed which negatively impacted our lives. While this could be true, the fact is that it is now a bygone and the best thing you can do is to forgive and forget. Every one of us makes mistakes and therefore we should not hold onto grudges for things that other people did to us. The more you hold on to a past mistake, the more you are cultivating an environment that promotes shifting of focus from your personal responsibility to pointing fingers on others.

Setting Personal Boundaries

As part of the process of taking responsibility, you should set boundaries that define who you are, what you believe in and the set of behaviors that are acceptable and unacceptable to you. Just like the way we set physical boundaries and put "No Trespassing" sign, we should also act in a similar manner towards our lives. Personal boundaries are important because they clearly demarcate where you end and where others begin.

Personal boundaries are not visible but rather determined largely by the emotional and physical space that you allow between your territory and that of others. They enable you to decide with finality the type of behavior, communication and interactions that you consider acceptable.

Types of Personal Boundaries

There are various types of personal boundaries and some of them are discussed below:

Physical Boundaries

These types of boundaries consist of a barrier between you and an intrusive force. They include your sense of personal space, your body and your sexual orientation. These boundaries are defined by the clothing you wear, your tolerance to noise, your shelter, body language and verbal instruction.

Emotional Boundaries

These boundaries are installed to protect your sense of personality and self-esteem. Weak emotional boundaries can expose you to emotional wounds and bruises through the words, actions and thoughts of other people. These boundaries are defined by your beliefs, choices, behaviors, sense of responsibility and your level of intimacy with other people.

Examples of emotional boundary invasions:

There are several ways in which your emotional boundaries can be invaded or violated. Some of them include:

- Codependency - This is where you allow the moods of others to dictate your emotions. It shows a clear lack of knowledge on how to separate your feelings from those of other people.

- Sacrificing to please others - Putting aside personal goals, dreams and ambitions in order to make other people happy is a sign of an invasion into your personal boundaries.

- Blaming other people for personal misfortunes - Taking responsibility for personal actions and choices is a sign of emotional intelligence and maturity. The moment you find yourself heaping blames on others, you should know that you are slowly punching holes on your emotional boundary.

Reasons behind the Invasion of Emotional Boundaries

There are various reasons that explain why our emotional boundaries are at times vulnerable to invasions and why we fail to uphold or enforce these boundaries.

- Fear of Rejection – Sometimes we open up our emotional boundaries to accommodate people because we fear being abandoned if we do not do so. This could be in a marital relationship, family or societal setting where you fear being rejected by your spouse, family members and the community respectively.

- Fear of Confrontation - The perception that you may end up in a confrontation with another person can send signals into your emotions to open up your emotional boundaries. This is where you find yourself agreeing with someone just for the sake of it so as to avoid an argument.

- Guilt - A guilt conscience can easily render you vulnerable to emotional invasions. When you do something wrong, the guilt that results from the action makes you defenseless and at times desperate.

- Lack of Knowledge - Setting healthy personal boundaries requires knowledge and some sort of training which can be formal or informal. If you are not aware of how these boundaries are set, then you are likely to be invaded by external forces.

Features of Healthy Personal Boundaries

- High Self-Esteem - People with healthy personal boundaries have a high perception of their abilities. They also have self respect which guides them when interacting with their environment.

- Gradual Sharing of Personal Information - If you have effective boundaries, you will tend to open up slowly as you learn about the other person and whether to trust them or not.

- Protection of Emotional and Physical Space - Strong personal boundaries will drive you into protecting your personal space from intrusion.

- Assertion - An effective personal boundary manifests itself in the form of self confidence. You will not be afraid to say no even if others are saying yes. Your decisions will be firm and you will be ready to stand by them.

- Taking Responsibility - Strong boundaries empower you to make healthy and responsible choices in life. You will not at any time push the blame onto others for something you are squarely responsible for.

Characteristics of Unhealthy Boundaries

Just like there are healthy boundaries, there are also unhealthy personal boundaries. The following features distinguish these kinds of boundaries.

- Revealing Too Much Information - There is a timeframe within which you are expected to reveal information about yourself. However due to unhealthy boundaries, we tend to share too much too soon.

- Living for Others - In as much as we are part of a society, every person should care about their needs first and then accommodate others. Feeling responsible for the happiness of others could be an indication that your personal boundaries are weak.

- Inability to Say No - Because of real or perceived fears, you may find yourself unable to raise an objection for something that you truly do not accept. This is a weakness and a typical feature of unhealthy boundaries.

- Disenfranchisement - At times we feel powerless in decision making and as such invite others unconsciously to rule our lives. This state of helplessness is caused by weak and porous personal boundaries.

How to Set Personal Boundaries

Now that you understand what personal boundaries are and the features that define healthy and unhealthy boundaries, it is important that you know the practical steps in setting up these boundaries.
Setting personal boundaries; emotional and physical, is a process that takes time and therefore needs patience.

Consider What Your Boundaries Are

It is almost impossible to create and enforce your boundaries if you are not aware of what they are. Take time to think about the things that make you comfortable and those that make you uncomfortable. Establish the extent to which others can come into your life and the things they should do as they approach you. This will help you draw clear lines that will define your boundaries.

Verbalize Your Needs

Do not be afraid to let others know of the things that you need. For instance, if someone is making noise, you should clearly tell them that you want silence and as such they should step back or go somewhere else far away from you. This will send a signal to inform them that they are intruding into your private space.

Put in Place Consequences

Just like with any boundary violation, there are always consequences that follow. Individuals can be experimental in that they can make a minor infraction to see whether there are any consequences. If no repercussions come up, they will continue intruding and even establish a new code of behavior towards you. You need to deliberately put in place consequences such as discontinuing a conversation, leaving the area or refuse to answer. This will ward others off.

Stand Your Ground

If you are to successfully create and maintain your personal boundaries, you must hold tight to your ideals and value system and not let them to slip off even for a minute. The moment you make a mistake and compromise your stand, then other people can swoop in and go ahead to violate your boundaries.

Emotional intelligence is reflected in how you take responsibility and define your personal space. A person with a clear value system and a set of identifiable boundaries is considered more responsible and emotionally intelligent.

5: The Importance of Meditation in Enhancing Emotional Intelligence

The impact of meditation in emotional intelligence is so profound that it cannot be ignored. Research has shown that meditation shapes the perception a person has of the world and how they evaluate their emotions. Whenever people face emotive issues either at the workplace or at a family level, meditation is one of the ways they can use to step back from the situation and look at it from an independent angle. This way, they are able to respond to the issue without emotions and as such stand a better chance of making a sober decision.

Components of Emotional Intelligence

John Mayer and Peter Salovey, leading researchers on emotional intelligence appreciate the role that meditation plays in enhancing emotional control. These two researchers developed a model which identified the key components of emotional intelligence which are:

- The ability to perceive emotions

- The capacity to reason using emotions

- The ability to comprehend and manage the impact of emotions

Meditation and the Perception of Emotions

Meditation gives you the capacity to observe and learn about emotions and thoughts. Instead of letting emotions impact your inner being negatively, meditation will help you to remove such emotions, thereby remaining sober and in control. In addition to comprehending your own thoughts, meditation enables you to understand the thoughts of others too. You will be able to read their facial expressions, verbal language, body language and the energy they project.

The Ability to Reason Using Emotions

Whenever we go through situations that are not pleasant, it is natural for us to feel a bit worked up. During such times, our response is fueled by our emotions. Meditation helps us to reason with our emotions. This means that when emotionally unsettling situations come our way, we will be in better position to condition our responses instead of getting caught in automatic and unconscious responses.

Reasoning using emotions is an indispensable aspect of interpersonal relationships that allows us to interact with others while at the same time being careful on how we respond to issues.

Meditation and Understanding of Emotions

Meditation enhances self-awareness thereby enabling us to interpret the cause of our emotions and those of others. Through meditation, we get the opportunity to open a dialogue inside us which helps us to get to the bottom of any incident. For instance, if someone cut you off in traffic, instead of throwing tantrums you can choose to analyze the situation and the possible reasons as to why the person decided to do whatever he did. It could be that he was distracted, under stress or totally unconscious of what he was doing. Meditation gives us a platform upon which we can analyze the behavior of others and decide on how to respond.

How Meditation Increases Emotional Intelligence

Through the engagement of both hemispheres of the brain, meditation can help in enhancing emotional intelligence and increase your memory.

Below are some of the ways through which meditation can achieves this.

Harnessing Your Brain Power

Research shows that most people use one side of the brain more than the other. This creates an imbalance which lowers our productivity and ability to consciously respond to issues. Through meditation, the two sides of the brain hemispheres are synchronized. This allows for faster neural communication and enhanced processing power.

Whenever the creative and logical sides of the brain work in harmony, problem solving becomes much easier and creativity is enhanced. This will enable you to concentrate and focus on issues thereby understanding them more.

Increases the Brain Size

Studies from the University of Wisconsin found that meditation increases the gray matter thickness of certain sections of the brain. In layman terms, this means that the brain becomes bigger, works faster and acts smarter. It is the same manner in which physical exercise makes your muscles denser, stronger and more enduring.

Although some scientific theories allege that intelligence is genetically linked, there are things we can do as human beings to enhance our brain performance. Meditation is one of those strategies you can use to increase intelligence in every aspect of your life.

Meditation Makes You Smarter

Meditation refines and directs your brainwave patterns into the most beneficial alpha, theta and delta frequencies. This brings on board a lot of benefits including powerful idea generation, super creativity, improved cognitive functioning and an overall boost in intellectual capacity for growth. Meditation is arguably the easiest route to accessing these super beneficial states of the mind which can tremendously transform your life in many different ways.

Development of Insight and Intuition

Your inner intelligence can be improved significantly by listening to the inner voice. Meditation gives you the key to unlocking the chambers of intuition and insight which are valuable in stimulating creativity and enhancing natural understanding of concepts and events. Insight and intuition also help you to visualize things that are far beyond your five senses.

Meditation Boosts both Short and Long Term Memory

Both emotional intelligence (EQ) and intelligence quotient (IQ) are subject to the memory. For you to function normally even in your day to day activities, having a memory that works right is essential. The two areas of the brain that are critical to memory; the frontal brain lobe and hippocampus show intense activity when a person is meditating. This means that meditation stimulates these vital areas thereby enhancing the long and short term capacity of the memory to grasp concepts and recall events. This makes your school work, your job and daily life much easier.

Meditation therefore plays a key role in making us emotionally intelligent. You can meditate in more than one way and it does not necessarily mean that you have to be in a given position for you to meditate. Some people meditate as they walk; others meditate while lying down while others meditate while listening to some soft music or travelling. This shows the dynamic nature of meditation. You can start small and gradually increase the number of hours under which you meditate. This will give you sanity of mind and purpose.

6: How to Raise Your Emotional Intelligence

The information that comes to our brain usually passes through our senses. Whenever this information is emotional or overwhelmingly stressful, our instincts take over and our capacity to act is limited to fight, flight, and freeze. In order to make good decisions when confronted with such situations, we need to deliberately balance our emotions.

Emotion is also linked strongly to memory. If you learn to stay connected to the emotional and rational part of your brain, you will be able to expand your range of choices when responding to a new event. In addition, integrating emotional memory into your decision making processes will prevent you from repeating earlier mistakes.

Key Skills of Emotional Intelligence

In order to improve your emotional intelligence and the ability to make sober decisions, you need to fully understand your emotions and how to manage them. To enable you do this, you have to develop key skills for managing and controlling your stress levels. These skills can be learned virtually by anyone who is willing to apply the knowledge they have learned into their lives.

In order to change your behavior permanently to enable you to withstand pressure, you need to learn how to overcome stress by maintaining emotional composure and awareness.

Rapid Stress Reduction

Stress is part of our day to day lives but when it comes at overwhelming levels, it can subdue the mind and the body. Stress also hinders us from communicating clearly and interferes with our ability to accurately read a situation. To remain focused, balanced and in control, you have to learn how to calm yourself down regardless of the level of stress that you are facing. Stress-busting is one of the techniques you can use to cope well amidst stressful events.

The following steps can help you to develop your stress-busting skills.

Be Aware of Your Physical Response to Stress

In order to control your emotions and reduce the impact of stress, you need to know how you physically respond to stressful events. Analyze carefully how your body feels when you are under stress because this will help you to regulate tension when it occurs.

People react differently to stress. While some become angry or agitated, others become withdrawn and depressed. If you tend to become angry when stressed, you will respond well to stress relieving events because they will quiet you down. On the other hand if stress depresses you, pursuing activities that are stimulating will be the best thing that will cheer you up.

Analyze the Stress-Busting Tactics that Work for You

One of the best ways to reduce stress quickly is through an engagement of your senses. Every person has their own way of responding to each of these sensory inputs and the secret lies in finding things that are energizing or soothing to you. For instance if you are a visual person, you can fight off stress by surrounding yourself with images that are uplifting. On the other hand, if you respond better to sound, you can get yourself a favorite piece of music to help you relax.

Emotional Awareness

The ability to connect with your emotions is critical to understanding yourself. It also helps you to be calm and focused even in situations that are tense. In the society today, many people are disconnected from their emotions because of negative childhood experiences that taught them to shut off their feelings when faced with stressful situations. The reality however is that, though we can deny, distort or numb our feelings, we cannot eliminate them. They still exist within us whether we acknowledge them or not.

Being emotionally unaware hinders our ability to fully understand our needs and motivations thereby putting us at a greater risk of becoming overwhelmed in threatening situations. For us to achieve emotional intelligence, we must reconnect with our emotions and accept them.

Emotional awareness can be learned and developed at any given time. Just like any development process, emotional awareness development needs to be gradual, starting with stress management and then reconnecting to stronger emotions afterwards. This will help you to change the way you experience emotions and how to respond to them.

Non-Verbal Communication

Effective communication is important in understanding and expressing our emotions. What you say may not be as important as how you say it. The non-verbal signals and gestures that accompany your communication and expressions help you to connect and establish trust with others. In addition, your ability to accurately read and respond to the non-verbal cues of others is important in interpersonal relationships.

Communication does not stop the moment someone stops speaking. On the contrary, even in silence non-verbal communication still continues. Ensure that what you say matches what you feel. Non-verbal messages can produce a sense of trust, interest, excitement and the desire for connection. On the other hand, these messages can also project a sense of fear, distrust, confusion and disinterest.

How to Improve Non-Verbal Communication

The success of non-verbal communication depends on your ability to recognize your emotions, manage stress and understand the signals that you are transmitting and receiving during communication.

Focus on the other party

By focusing on the person you are communicating with, you will be able to decode any non-verbal cues that can help you to plan what to say next.

Make eye contact

Eye contact is important in communicating interest, gauging the other person's response and maintaining the conversation flow.

Be conscious of the non-verbal cues you are sending

Signals such as facial expression, gesture, posture and the tone of your voice speaks a lot to the other person regarding your feelings and emotions.

Using Humor and Play to Deal with Challenges

Laughter, humor and play are antidotes to difficulties that you may encounter in life. They help in lightening your burdens and fixing your focus on the things ahead. It is scientifically proven that laughter reduces stress, balances your nervous system and elevates your mood. Playful communication can help you to:

- Gain a new perspective - Hardships comes to every one of us in one form or another.

Humor and laughter allows you to view your disappointments and frustrations from a totally new angle. This in turn enables you to survive annoyances, setbacks and hard times.

- Smooth over disagreements - Even though parties to a conversation may disagree on a certain issue, humor allows you to express your opinion without creating a flap.

- Relax and energize - Playful communication can relieve your body and mind of fatigue and subsequently relax them. This gives you the opportunity to recharge and get ready to accomplish even more things.

- Become more creative - Humor frees you up from your rigid ways of perceiving things thereby allowing you to be more creative when engaging in events.

In light of these benefits of humor and playful communication, you should consider developing and embracing humor in your conversations. You can achieve this in a simple way by setting aside quality play time. The more you play, joke and laugh, the more you become less stressed and therefore become an effective communicator.

You can also find activities that help you to loosen and embrace your playful nature. You can start by playing with young children, animals and other outgoing people who appreciate play as an important part of their lives.

Resolve Conflict Positively

In relationships, disagreements and conflicts are inevitable. People have different opinions, needs and expectations that always put them in conflict with others. Resolving conflict in a healthy and constructive manner can therefore help in strengthening the bond of relationship between worrying parties. Conflict resolution as a skill helps in fostering safety, creativity and freedom in relationships.

Tips for Resolving Conflict

The following tips can help you to resolve conflict:

Staying focused in the present

Holding on to old resentments can hinder you from recognizing the reality of a current situation and thereby miss the opportunity for resolving old conflicts and feelings. You need to stay focused and treat every situation as a new chance to make up for old grudges.

Choose Your Arguments

Arguments take energy and time to resolve. This means that you should carefully consider if something is worth arguing about.

Forgive

Forgiveness is the best approach to resolving hurtful behaviors of the past. In order to amicably resolve a conflict, you need to give up the urge to seek revenge or punish.

Choose to end conflicts

Disagreements that cannot be resolved should be terminated so that focus can be on other important things. Even if you disagree on a matter, you can still disengage and move on with life.

Emotional intelligence can therefore be raised through the strategies and steps highlighted above. The more you practice these strategies, the more intelligent you become emotionally.

7: Keys to Commanding Your Emotions

If you master your emotions, you will master your life. It is important to understand the reason as to why we do things is because of an inner desire to change the way we feel. For instance, if you want to lose weight, make more money or buy new clothes, you are doing this precisely because of the feeling that you will get when you achieve your goal. People who believe that by losing weight they will become more confident, they will be able to attract the person they love into their life, will make every effort to shed off the extra pounds.

Emotions are very important components of our lives. Instead of putting them off, we should acknowledge them and realize the truth that lies in them.

The Emotional Triad

There are three main factors that determine your feelings regardless of the situation you are in. Psychologists call these factors the Emotional Triad. They include:

Your Physiology

Every kind of emotion that you experience in your life is first and foremost felt in your body. For instance, if you want to feel more confident, then you should be grounded, principled and courageous in your speech. On the other hand, if you want to feel passionate, you should start by speaking and moving more rapidly. For those people who for one reason or another want to feel depressed, all they need to do is to frown, breathe shallowly, slump over and look at the ground. The bottom line here is that the manner in which you use your body changes how you feel. Emotion is created by motion.

What You Focus On

Apart from your physiology, what you focus on also determines how you feel. To feel happy, you need to focus on things that will make you happy. By remembering happy moments from the past, you can create a platform and an opportunity for you to be happy today.

When you delete all the good things and experiences and instead focus on the negative, you will certainly get depressed. In life, both good things and bad things are always available and it is upon you to decide where your focus is going to be.

Your Language

Whatever words you use have the capacity to change the way you feel. If you start making statements like "I really feel tired" or "I am bored", chances are that you will feel tired. Every word that you utter has an emotional state attached to it. Some words are disempowering while others are encouraging and uplifting. By exercising care over your vocabulary, metaphors, statements and phrases, you can control and command your emotions.

The reality brought to you by the Emotional Triad is that happiness is a choice and the same goes for anger, depression and frustration. There is no one who makes you feel angry or happy; rather it all depends on how you interpret each situation in your life.

How to Deal With Negative Emotions

As mentioned earlier, negative and positive emotions are part of our lives and we cannot just wish them away. However, you can decide to deal with such emotions so as to suppress the negative ones and encourage the positive. There are four ways through which people deal with negative emotions.

Avoidance

Avoidance means keeping away from all situations that have the potential to lead you into negative emotions. For instance, some people may avoid approaching strangers or taking risks because of the fear of rejection or failure. It is common to see people self-medicating themselves with alcohol, drugs or food so as to ward off negative emotions. This is another form of avoidance.

Denial

Denial is the process of dissociating yourself from negative emotions by using statements such as, "It wasn't that bad". While it may seem to be perfectly okay for you to go into denial, the only problem with this approach is that the emotion will increase because you constantly ignore it. It will intensify until you finally pay attention.

Learning and Using Your Negative Emotions

Learning from your negative emotions and using them to serve you is one of the ways used to deal with negative emotions. As a first step, you need to understand that all emotions are there to serve you. Your negative emotions are action signals that notify you of something. The emotions that you feel daily in your life are a guideline, a gift, a support system or a call to action. They tell you that the activity you are in does not and will not work.

The key thing to remember is that you are the origin of all your emotions and you are the only one who creates them. You do not need a special reason to feel a certain way but rather it is all your choice.

The Steps to Emotional Mastery

In order to command your emotions, you need to take deliberate steps. Below is a procedure that you can use to achieve this.

Identify Your Real Feelings

Every time you feel a negative emotion, you should ask yourself what it is that you are exactly feeling. Get a clear picture of your emotions.

Acknowledge and Appreciate Your Emotions

Your emotion is your support system and you should be thankful for the action signals. Deliberately cultivate a sense of appreciation for all the emotions that you feel. They are there to serve you and not the other way round.

Get Curious About the Message Transmitted by the Emotions

By getting curious, you will master your emotions and solve the challenge faster and easier. You will also bar the same emotions from recurring in the future.

Be Confident

Confidence is very important in overcoming and controlling your emotions. As a matter of fact, it is one of the easier ways to handle any emotion. All you need to do is just remember similar emotional instances in the past and what you did to overcome them. If you triumphed in the past, you should tap into that confidence to help you handle your emotions today.

This confidence should also extend into the future. You should be optimistic that you can manage future emotional experiences because you did it in the past.

Get Excited and Take Action

When faced with an emotion, the first step is to be confident that you are able to handle it and take immediate action. The best time to handle any emotion is the moment you first begin to experience it. Mastering your emotions takes time and practice. It is therefore important that you learn to be patient.

The Action Signals

Every negative emotion, also referred to as action signal has a message that is trying to pass on to us. Our responsibility therefore, is to identify the message and use it to better assist us. Some of the common signals include:

Discomfort

Also known as impatience, boredom, uneasiness or mild embarrassment, discomfort is an action signal that tells you that you can be more than what you are currently. This means that you need to change your perception or your actions. You can use the Emotional Triad discussed above to change your state or clarify what you want. You should also refine your actions and try a different approach in order to see whether it will change the way you feel about the situation at hand.

Fear

Fear is also referred to as intense worry, low levels of concern, terror or fright. The message that fear brings to us is that something is going to happen soon and we need to be prepared for it. This is good because the fear action signal gives us massive energy to prepare. Whenever fear starts to creep in, you need to immediately review the substance of the fear and evaluate the things you must do to prepare yourself psychologically. To antidote your fear, you need to make a deliberate decision of faith by telling yourself that all is prepared and you have no reason to worry.

Hurt

This is a sense of loss or an expectation that is unmet. The message that we can decode from hurt is that of a lost intimacy or trust. To solve and erase any hurt feelings, you need to realize that you have not necessarily lost anything and what you need to actually lose is the false perception that is haunting you. You can also re-evaluate the situation to see whether there is any real loss or you are just judging the situation too harshly or too soon. By communicating your feelings appropriately with the person involved, you can take control of any hurtful feeling.

Anger

Anger is a feeling of irritation, resentment, rage or fury. The message we learn from anger is that an important standard or rule that we hold dear in our lives has been violated either by another person or ourselves. Anger gives you the firepower you need to make things right.

To take control of anger, you should realize that you may have interpreted the situation wrongly or that the person breaking your rules may not be aware of how they are important to you. You should also consider the fact that your rules may not be necessarily right that is why they were violated in the first instance.

Frustration

The frustration action signal originates from the brain and it means that you are currently operating below capacity. The solution may be within range but the things you are currently doing are not working right and therefore you need to change your approach. Frustrations are also a signal that you need to be more flexible in your approach. To command frustration emotions, you need to brainstorm different options available to get the desired results. Getting a role model who has succeeded in the things you are struggling with is also important because their input can help you in dealing with the situation.

Disappointment

This is a feeling that comes when you are let down or you are sad. If you have an expectation that probably isn't going to happen and you are forced to change your approach, you could be disappointed. Instead of wallowing in self pity, you should immediately figure out the things you can learn from the situation, set new goals and realize that there is a probability that you may be judging too soon. You need to realize that the situation is not over as yet and you should develop more patience and cultivate a positive expectancy attitude.

Guilt

Guilt is an action signal also known as regret or remorse. It is an indication that you have violated one of your central standards and that you must do something to ensure that the standard is not violated again. Instead of taking guilt negatively, appreciate it as an internal compass that helps you to do what you believe is right. To solve guilt, you need to acknowledge that you indeed have violated a critical standard. In addition, you should commit yourself to ensure that the violation will never happen again both in the near and distant future.

Inadequacy

As an action signal, inadequacy is a feeling of unworthiness that comes when we are unable to do something that we are capable of doing. The message this action signal gives us is that we do not have the skills needed to perform the task before us. It also indicates that we need more understanding, information, tools or confidence. The good thing with this feeling is that it pushes us to grow, learn and contribute to others. The first step in tackling inadequacy is to ask yourself whether you need to change your perception or not. You should also understand that you are not perfect but rather a work in progress. A role model who can coach you is also an invaluable resource.

The power to commanding your emotions lies within you. Every emotion comes from you and you are the only one who is best suited to handle and subdue it. With continual practice, you can take advantage of these emotions to work to your advantage.

8: Emotional control and anger management

Do you find yourself in frequent arguments and fights? This could be as a result of anger. Anger is a healthy and normal emotion but when it reaches chronic levels, it can be explosive and spiral out of control. This may bring serious consequences in your relationships, your state of mind and even your health. Getting insights about anger management tools and the real reasons behind your anger can help you to learn how to keep your temper from hijacking your life.

Understanding Anger

The anger emotion is neither good nor bad. It is normal and healthy to display it when you have been wronged or mistreated. While the feeling is not the problem, what you do with it makes a whole lot of difference. It has the potential to harm you and other people as well.

Most people believe that when they have a hot temper, their ability to control their anger is at its lowest. The reality however is that we have more control over anger than we imagine. You can learn to express your emotions freely without hurting other people and in doing this you will feel much better and your needs will be met faster. Mastering the art of anger management is not an easy task but the more you practice it, the higher the likelihood of it becoming much easier. Anger management affects your relationships, goal achievement and your level of satisfaction in life.

Misconceptions about Anger

There are several things that we hold as true which in real sense are false. Below is an exposition of some of the misconceptions about anger and anger management.

It Is Healthy to Vent out Anger

While it is true that ignoring and suppressing anger is unhealthy, letting it out is not any better. Anger is not supposed to be let out in an aggressive manner because this can blow you up. Tirades and outbursts only serve to fuel the fire and reinforce the magnitude of your anger.

Aggression and anger can Earn You Respect

True power does not come through bullying of others. People may fear you but it does not mean that they respect you. Controlling yourself amidst opposing viewpoints is one of the ways to display emotional maturity. If you train yourself to communicate in a respectful way, you will gain the favor of others and many people will be more willing to listen and accommodate your views.

Anger Is Not Something You Can Control

People who are at the verge of giving up quickly conclude that anger cannot be controlled. The reality is that we cannot control every situation that comes our way but we can control the way we respond and express our feelings. It is possible to express anger without being physically or verbally abusive. Even if someone is pushing you to the corner, you can choose how you want to respond.

Anger Management Is All About Learning How to Suppress Your Anger

Anger is a normal behavioral response and will come out regardless of how hard we try to suppress it. Anger control has everything to do with becoming aware of your underlying feelings and developing healthier ways on how to manage upsets. Instead of trying to suppress your anger, your goal should be to express it in a constructive way.

The Importance of Anger Management

While many people think that they have every right to vent their anger and that the people who surround them are being overly sensitive, the truth is that anger is damaging to relationships and impairs judgment. Emotional outbursts have always gotten in the way of success and have a negative impact on how people perceive you.

When anger spirals out of control, it hurts even your own physical health. Operating constantly at high levels of tension and stress is not good for your health. Scientific research has shown that chronic anger makes you more vulnerable to heart diseases, high cholesterol levels, diabetes, insomnia, a weakened immune system and high blood pressure.

When we are angry, we tend to consume huge amounts of mental energy and this has the potential of crowding our thinking. This in turn makes it increasingly difficult and harder for us to concentrate, see the big picture ahead and enjoy life. Stress, depression and other mental problems are common in people who experience frequent cycles of anger.

Out of control anger can affect the success of your career. Even though creative differences, constructive criticism and heated debates are healthy, lashing out can potentially alienate your supervisors, colleagues or clients further leading to an erosion of respect. More to this, a bad reputation will follow you in every place that you go.

Anger can be so dangerous as to cause scars in people that you relate and care about This ruins relationships and friendships. Very few people if any will trust you, feel comfortable while with you or speak honestly about issues that affect you because they never know how you will respond. Parents with explosive anger can affect their children psychologically.

Anger Management Tips

Having seen the importance of managing your anger and not letting it spiral out of control, we need to now focus on how to manage anger using a few workable and practical tips.

Understand the Cause of Your Anger

Nothing comes our way without a cause. There must be an underlying issue that makes you struggle out of control. Most of the problems that made you angry usually stem from the things you learned when you were a small child. For instance, if you grew up in a family where every member was violent against the other, you might have picked a notion that anger is supposed to be used as a tool of expression to get everything your way. High levels of stress and traumatic events could also be some of the underlying factors that make you susceptible to anger.

Some people use anger as a cover up for feelings such as insecurity, embarrassment, vulnerability, hurt or shame. This means that such people are not truly angry but rather connect to certain events that make them angry. Normally, knee-jerk responses are evidence that the temper expressed is just but a cover up for other feelings and needs. This happens mostly in families where anger was highly discouraged.

Beware of Your Anger Triggers and Warning Signs

Every build up of an anger explosion is characterized by warning signs. As a matter of fact, some of these signs are physical in nature and are manifested through your body. Anger fuels the fight or flight system of your body and the angrier you get, the more the chances of your body going into an overdrive. The moment you take time to study the warning system of your body, you can effectively manage your temper before it goes out of control.

It is easy to point a finger on others and blame them for the circumstances around you while forgetting that the real cause of your anger is you and how you respond to situations. It has very little if anything to do with the actions of others. Negative thought patterns can trigger anger. Some of these patterns include:

- Over-generalizing – Using blanket statements such as "you always mistreat me", "you are never concerned with my welfare", "everyone thinks bad about me" and many more can fuel anger and resentment.

- Premature evaluations - Jumping into conclusions about how other people behave towards us can also be a source of anger. For instance, you may think that someone has intentionally ignored you while in real sense, they had not seen you.

- Collecting straws - If you constantly look for things to make you upset, you will surely become angry. When the small irritations that you entertain build up, they have a capacity to make you explode even over something that is very minor.

Learn Ways to Cool Down

There are many techniques you can use to help you cool down and keep your anger in control. Some of these techniques include:

- Counteract rising tension with a deep breath - By taking a deep and slow breath from the abdomen, you can get as much fresh air as possible which will help you to ease tension.

- Exercise - Taking a walk is also a good idea because it releases pent up energy that helps you approach a situation with a cooler head.

- Make Use of Your Senses - By taking advantage of the relaxing power of your sense of smell, sight, touch, sound and taste, you are able to calm down easily.

- Massaging or stretching the tension areas - Massage helps in relieving tension in all areas that it has built up. For instance, stretching or massaging your shoulders, your neck and your scalp can help your body to relax and ease tension.

- Remove yourself from the situation - Any time you find your anger spiraling out of control, one of the things you can do to calm down is to remove yourself from the situation. This helps you to release tension and gives you space to reconsider your response.

Seeking Professional Help

If you have practiced anger management on your own without success, it is important that you seek the help of an expert. There are therapies, programs and classes that are designed for people who have anger management problems. Asking for help is never a sign of weakness but rather a willingness on your part to find a solution to your problem. You will find many other people who suffer from the same problems and together you can help one another overcome this problem.

9: Emotional Intelligence and Conflict Resolution

Every relationship has its ups and downs and conflict is an inherent component. As a matter of fact, no two people can agree on everything every time. There must be an instance or two when their preferences differ. Learning how to handle conflict rather than wishing it away is crucial and the epitome of emotional intelligence. Whenever conflict is mismanaged, chances of it causing great harm to a relationship are very high. However, when it is handled in a positive and respective manner, it can create opportunities for strengthening relationship bonds. Learning conflict resolution skills is vital for keeping your professional and personal relationships strong.

Understanding the Cause of Conflict in relationships

Conflict can arise from both large and small differences between individuals. Whenever people disagree over motivations, values, ideas, perceptions or desires, they are bound to enter into a conflict. A conflict could be fueled by trivial differences but at the center of it, there is usually a deeper personal need. The needs can range from safety to respect and anything in between.

Conflict can arise from both large and small problems. Whenever people disagree over their perceptions, motivations, values, ideas or desires there is bound to be conflict. While some of the differences at times are minor, deep personal needs can cause conflicts that trigger strong feelings. These needs can range from security to respect and intimacy plus anything in between.

Conflicts Arising From Differing Needs

Every person has a desire within them to feel nurtured, understood and supported. While these needs may seem similar, the ways in which they are met varies from person to person.

The need for safety and continuity often conflicts with the need to explore. This type of conflict is always seen between children and their parents. The children want to take risks and explore while the parents are concerned and want them to be safe above everything else. Setting a limit to the exploration thus becomes the bone of contention between the two parties.

The needs expressed by both parties are vital and necessary for the long-term success of the relationship. In interpersonal relationships, a misunderstanding of differing needs can lead to arguments and breakups. At the workplace, such conflicts can result into broken deals, bitter disputes, lost jobs and fewer profits. The moment you recognize the legitimacy of varying and conflicting needs, then a pathway must be created in order to solve the problem, improve relationships and engage in team building.

How to Perceive Conflict

People perceive conflict differently. There are those who avoid conflicts because of the painful memories associated with them. If you previously had unhealthy relationships, your perception of conflict could be that it all ends up in disagreements. Conflict in relationships is at times viewed as being humiliating, demoralizing, dangerous, or even something to be feared. In the event you had childhood experiences that left you powerless or feeling out of control, conflict may traumatize you.

If you view conflict as being dangerous, then most often than not your prophesy will be self-fulfilled. If you go into a conflict while feeling threatened, it becomes difficult to handle the conflict in a healthy manner. There is a high probability that you will shut down or even blow up in anger.

Conflict Resolution, Emotions and Stress

Stress makes it very difficult to understand your own needs which in turn will give you a hard time in communicating those needs of other people. It is always important that you maintain calmness of the mind whenever you are resolving a conflict. This will make it easy to express your feelings to others in a manner that they can appreciate them. Your ability to resolve conflict will depend on:

- Your ability to manage stress in a calm and effective way. If you remain calm in a conflict, you will have the advantage of reading and interpreting both verbal and non-verbal communication.

- Your ability to control your behaviors and emotions. By being in control of your emotions, you will be able to communicate your needs without frightening, threatening or punishing others.

- Your ability to respect differences. Avoiding disrespectful actions and words can help you to solve a problem much faster than it would have been the case.

Conflict Resolution Skills

In order to successfully resolve a conflict, you should practice two core skills. The first one is the ability to quickly reduce stress while the second is the ability to remain comfortable with your emotions so as to react in constructive ways amidst arguments or perceived attacks.

Quick Stress Relief

Your ability to manage and relieve stress is important if you are to stay balanced and focused irrespective of the challenges that you face. The moment you fail to stay centered and in control of yourself, chances are that you will become overwhelmed in situations of conflict. This will affect the quality of your response.

Connie Lillas, a psychologist, used a driving analogy to describe the ways in which people respond when they are overwhelmed by stress.

- Foot on the gas - This is an agitated or angry stress response. It makes you overly emotional, heated, hyped up and unable to maintain calmness.

- Foot on the brake - This is a depressed or withdrawn stress response. In this condition, you space out, shut down and show very little emotion or energy.

- Foot on both gas and brake - This analogy describes a frozen or tense stress response. While you look paralyzed, under the surface you are extremely agitated.

If you often feel tight or tense somewhere in your body or conflict absorbs most of your attention or time, then stress is a major problem in your life.

Emotional awareness

Emotional awareness helps you to understand yourself and others too. If you do not know how you feel, you will not be able to resolve conflicts amicably. This is because conflict resolution calls for effective communication. Knowing your feelings may sound like a simple process but the reality is that many people ignore strong emotions such as sadness, anger and fear. Your connection to these feelings will determine how you handle conflict. If you are afraid of strong emotions, then your ability to resolve differences in a conflict will be impaired.

Conflict Resolution and Non-Verbal Communication

During conflicts, the most important information is usually exchanged non-verbally. This can be done by emotionally driven facial expressions, gesture, posture, pace, intensity of voice and tone.

Whenever people are angry, the words they use hardly convey the deep issues of their heart. In order to connect with their feelings, you need to listen to what is being said in addition to what is being felt. This kind of listening informs us, strengthens us and makes it a little bit easier for other people to hear us.

In the midst of a conflict, paying close attention to the non-verbal communication expressed by the other person can help you in figuring out what they are really saying. This will allow you to respond in a manner that builds trust and helps you to get to the root of the problem. A reassuring touch, a calm voice or a concerned facial expression can go a long way into enabling a tense exchange.

Emotionally intelligent people have higher chances of success in resolving conflicts because they can position themselves in the shoes of either party in order to feel where it pinches.

10: Mastering Interpersonal Skills for Emotional Intelligence

Interpersonal skills are a great asset to anyone who is seeking career growth. It is what distinguishes great people from ordinary individuals. People who have excellent interpersonal skills are treated as being emotionally intelligent and friendly to be with.

It is possible to learn these soft skills and use them to improve the way in which you communicate and associate with other people. This chapter discusses the top must-have interpersonal skills.

Verbal Communication

Verbal communication is the most used form of self expression. We react to situations around us and communicate our emotions through the words that we speak. For others to understand us, we should ensure that our verbal communication pathway is clear. One of the easiest ways of developing clarity is by speaking more thoughtfully. While there is always the urge to respond to conversations and questions hastily you should pause for a moment to consider your response. The more thoughtful you become, the more measured your responses will be and people will respect you for that.

Verbal communication therefore needs a lot of calmness, politeness, focus and a level of interest necessary to match the emotion or mood of the situation.

Non-Verbal Communication

This type of communication is often underestimated and underrated. Non-verbal communication has a tremendous impact in that it reinforces what you are expressing verbally. It is possible to express an emotion or respond to a conversation without necessarily saying a single word.

Whether we are aware or not, non-verbal communication is something that people we interact with notice. Your body language constantly says something about your feelings. The way you position yourself in a room, your gestures, your voice and your posture reveals your attitude to the people around you. The bottom-line here is to learn how to interpret the body language of other people while at the same time learning how to perfect your own non-verbal communication pathway.

Listening

Listening is an indispensable personal skill that enables us to interpret and respond appropriately in conversations. Where listening is not effective, messages can be easily misunderstood, communication can breakdown and the sender can be frustrated.

Considering that good listening skills can enhance productivity, boost customer satisfaction and increase sharing of information, it is important that you make a deliberate effort to learn these skills.

There is a difference between listening and hearing; whereas hearing is concerned with the sounds that come into your ears, listening goes beyond that. It involves paying attention to the story, listening to the choice of words and how the other person in the conversation uses their body language. Your listening ability is determined to a greater extent by the degree in which you perceive and understand the message being presented.

Research shows that on average we spend more time listening than speaking, reading or writing. 70 percent of our time is spent in conversations and out of this, 45 percent is spent listening, 30 percent speaking, 16 percent reading and 9 percent writing.

Effective listening requires that you concentrate and use your other senses other than sound.

Principles of Listening

A good listener pays attention not only to verbal but also non-verbal communication. There are principles that you can adopt to make you a good listener and by extension an effective communicator.

- Stop talking - In the words of Mark Twain, "If we were supposed to talk more than we listen, we would have two tongues and one ear." Good listeners do less of talking and spend most of their time listening. Whenever a person is talking, take time to listen to what they are saying. Do not interrupt them but rather allow them to conclude their statements. In case you want to seek any clarifications, wait until they finish talking.

- Prepare Yourself to Listen - Effective listening needs a good internal and external environment. You should be relaxed, focused on the speaker and free from distractions. By blocking things out of your mind, you will create a good environment to concentrate on.

- Remove any Distractions - avoid behaviors that will disrupt your listening process such as shuffling of papers, doodling, picking your fingernails and looking out the window. Distractions interfere with the listening process and send messages to the other person that you have no such interest in the substance of the discussion.

- Empathize - During the listening process, try to understand the view and perspective of the other person. Do not enter into a conversation with preconceived ideas but rather have an open mind that appreciates the message being communicated. If you do not agree with part of the information, construct your argument properly while being tolerant to the opinions and views of others.

- Be patient - Patience is an invaluable component of listening that you cannot be without it. Be patient with the speaker and understand that a pause does not necessarily mean that they have finished speaking. It could be that they are reflecting or even recalling information to support the concept they are developing. Patience is also a gesture that you respect and value the information coming in from the speaker.

- Listen to the tone - Tone variation is a good indicator of the level of emotion in a conversation. A good speaker will often use tone and volume to grasp the attention of the audience. As a listener you need to carefully consider the tone of the message and the significance it has in the conversation.

Questioning

In the society we live in, questioning seems to be a lost art despite being an effective technique that builds on listening. Contrary to what many people believe, questioning is not just a tool for obtaining information but rather an excellent way to initiate conversation. Questioning demonstrates that you have interest in the subject matter being discussed. Asking smart questions demonstrates that you know how to approach problems in order to get the answers that you need. Questioning is among the easiest interpersonal skills to learn.

The quality of questioning is also important. If you ask closed type of questions, you will get closed answers. Open questions on the other hand explore further and open the conversation for a deeper level of engagement.

Problem solving

Life is a chain of problems that require solutions. The problems do not have to be negative in nature. As a matter of fact, anything that requires a solution is a problem. The speed in which you solve the problem is not as important as how you solve it. In problem solving, there is no plan that guarantees you success 100 percent. There is always an element of risk.

The key components of problem solving involves being able to identify and pinpoint the problem, dissecting it in order to fully understand it, examining the options that pertain to the solutions, coming up with strategies and objectives on how to solve the problem and putting the plan into action while monitoring progress.

Social Awareness

Being in tune with the needs and emotions of others is an essential interpersonal skill. Social awareness makes us embrace and appreciate the success of others. In addition, this skill helps us to identify opportunities around us. Being able to appropriately respond to a social situation is a clear demonstration that you are operating at a higher level of emotional intelligence and social awareness.

Self Management

Self management refers to the ability to control your emotions even when they are not aligned with what would be generally considered the appropriate behaviors in a given situation. Self management will enable you to control anger, hide frustrations and exude calmness. There is always the temptation to show your true colors and display your objection publicly but remaining calm and composed is oftentimes a desired course of action. It also shows emotional maturity.

Responsibility and Accountability

This set of interpersonal skills can easily help you to win the trust and confidence of other people. Responsibility means standing by what you say until your mission is accomplished. Making a promise and delivering on time is the epitome of responsibility.

Everybody would love to be accountable, but the truth is that there is always a price to pay. Not all things that we are to be accountable for are pleasant in nature. Some are shameful and disgraceful but that does not give us an excuse to avoid them. As long as they fall within our jurisdiction, we are to stand up and own them.

Assertiveness

The 21st century is arguably one of the most competitive both at the social and professional scene. Every person is trying all they can to put themselves ahead of the rest. Being assertive has oftentimes been confused with being overly aggressive and carefree; nothing can be further from the truth.

Assertiveness means standing up for what you believe and defending your course with confidence. For instance, if you feel that your current salary is not sufficient, you should not shy away from asking for a raise as long as it is justified. When used tactfully, assertiveness can help you gain a kind of respect that is unattainable by other means.

A well-balanced cocktail of interpersonal skills will allow you to handle any situation that comes your way gracefully. No one is accomplished when it comes to learning these skills. The more you press on the better you become in each of these skills.

11: How to Improve Your Emotional Health

In order to better relate to people and gain support when expressing your feelings, you need to control your emotions and behavior. People who are emotionally healthy are better prepared to handle life's challenges and build stronger relationships. Just as it takes time to build and maintain your physical health, it also takes time to improve your mental and emotional health. Emotional health helps you to build tenacity and resilience, boost your mood and enhance the quality of life.

What Is Emotional Health

Also known as mental health, emotional health refers to your entire psychological well-being. It encompasses the way you feel about yourself, your ability to manage your emotions and the quality of your relationships.

Emotionally healthy people have a sense of commitment, know how to deal with difficulties and stress in life, are flexible enough to learn new things, can balance work and play effectively and have a capacity to build and maintain relationships that are fulfilling.

How Your Physical Health Impacts Your Emotional Health

While physical health seems tangible and emotional health intangible, there is a thread that connects the two. The absence of one affects the other adversely. Taking care of your physical health is one of the surest ways of boosting your mental well-being. For instance, exercise strengthens our lungs and heart but also releases powerful chemicals known as endorphins which energize us and help in lifting our moods.

Some of the principles of physical health that can enhance your emotional health include:

Getting Enough Rest

For you to function optimally, you need to get adequate rest. This enables your body to relax and rejuvenate so you can get ready for the next round of activities. Resting is also one of the recommended ways to get rid of stress.

Practice Good Nutrition

Good nutrition is essential in maintaining both physical and emotional health. There are foods that can help you boost your energy and balance your moods.

Exercise Regularly

Exercising is powerful and it can help alleviate anxiety, stress and depression. Use every opportunity available in order to exercise. For instance, instead of taking the elevator when going to work, you can decide to use the stairs. To optimize your mental health through exercise, aim for workouts that last up to 30 minutes or more.

Enhancing Emotional Health through Supportive Relationships

The company of others is very important in enhancing your emotional and mental health. People are social creatures with a need for positive connections to others. In isolation, we can neither survive nor thrive.

When looking for supportive relationships, get in touch with people who have time to listen to you. Face to face conversations are very important because they help you express yourself and get instant feedback either verbally or non-verbally from the other person.

In order to connect with others, you need to spend time with the people you like, volunteer in activities that benefit other people and join special interest groups or social actions. In these groups, it will be easy for you to find people who you can share common interests.

Seek Professional Help

There are professionals who can help you to improve your emotional health. Their experience and knowledge is invaluable and will motivate you to do things that you previously were unable to. Do not shy away from opening up because it is only in doing so that you can get help and enhance your mental health.

Conclusion

Emotional intelligence is an interesting subject because it teaches and trains us to better relate with other people. With the pace at which the world is fast becoming a global village, it is essential that you learn how to listen and interpret information coming to you from others. This will in turn help you in structuring your response.

While many people confuse emotional intelligence and intelligence quotient, this book makes it clear that intelligence quotient is a subset of emotional intelligence. When you learn how to command your emotions, you will exercise more control over your life and unlock opportunities that would have otherwise remained hidden. Emotional maturity is something that every one of us is working towards attaining. This means that you should not be discouraged and sidetracked but rather press on and aggressively pursue your emotional goals to their final end.

CPSIA information can be obtained
at www.ICGtesting.com
Printed in the USA
LVOW04s1234171215

466988LV00018B/691/P

9 781505 442960